A Christmas Passing

A Christmas Passing

Sylvia Casberg

Sunny Fields Publishing

PO Box 546, Solvang, CA 93464-0546

Book design by Sylvia Casberg

First edition

ISBN 978-0-557-69394-8

Preface

When Christmas advertising begins in October and lasts through January sales, it's easy to lose sight of the true spirit of the season. Sometimes it is the small and simple stories that bring us back to the joy at the heart of Christmas.

A Christmas Passing is such a story.

It begins with an unexpected death, only a few days before Christmas. The grieving family gathers, and together they experience a Christmas none of them will ever forget, a Christmas filled with the healing power of community and family, laughter and tears.

A Christmas Passing is a story to share with the people you love.

For my children,
Michael and Nica
Melani and Chris
and my grandson, Gabriel

Introduction

Christmas stories can be magical. The smallest fir tree is chosen for the great hall. Scrooge turns into "Father Christmas." Dark nights are lit with one candle. Adults listen to small children. Sadness smiles in spite of itself.

This is the blessed irony of Christmas. And this is the story of **A Christmas Passing.**

Sylvia Casberg

A Christmas Passing

When the phone rings after midnight, I prepare myself for a birth, an accident or a death.

It is December 20th, 1:45 a.m. The voice on the line, choking with emotion, announces the sudden death of my husband's eldest brother.

By eight o'clock the next morning we have our plane tickets booked, our suitcases packed and someone to feed the dog.

$\sim$

We doze on the five-hour flight listening to Christmas carols, and land on time. The sun is just setting.

The youngest brother meets us at the luggage carousel and helps us to his car. He doesn't talk much, and when he does, his voice sounds strained.

We ask how the widow is doing and he tells us the whole family is at the house drinking coffee and passing around fresh baked biscuits with butter and honey.

Certain things are baked at certain times. Homemade biscuits keep body and soul together, especially the soul.

It will take a couple of hours to drive from the Raleigh-Durham Airport to Shannon. Teenagers make it in an hour or so, but this evening it is dark, the streets are narrow and we don't feel like teenagers.

$\sim$

We stop at the Peanut Roaster before getting on the road. The young man who runs the business is a friend of two of the cousins. His dad died earlier this year, so he runs the store alone.

Well, not quite alone. Cocoa, his chocolate-brown lab, handles customer relations: he sits up, gives you "five," and opens his mouth to be tossed peanuts.

My aim is not what it used to be, which gets me slobbered on so thoroughly I have to go to the ladies' room to wash up.

The sick leave policy posted on the bathroom door reminds workers:

> *"If you are well enough to go to the doctor, you are well enough to come to work, and if you are thinking of an operation, better think twice. Anyone who works here needs all their parts."*

We buy chocolate covered peanuts, southern fried peanuts – some with hard, red sugar coating – and a couple Diet Cokes to wash it all down.

~

The Carolina countryside is quiet and dark. Here and there Christmas lights sparkle through the pines and dried underbrush. We talk family talk and eat peanuts, eat more peanuts and talk more about the family.

By the time we get to the funeral home, canker sores from all that sugar are teasing my tongue along the insides of both cheeks. I don't know why I do this. It happens every time.

The hometown family is there ahead of us, greeting friends and relatives they haven't seen since the Thanksgiving potluck. Real old folks are helped down to the front seats. Here they sit on rickety metal folding chairs, with cardboard funeral home fans lying in their laps. They talk about Norman.

"Only sixty-one!"

"Much too young to die."

"How hard it is to lose him!"

"He was an institution."

I see so many faces and hear so many names, they soon blend into one long southern drawl, so I just stand quietly by my husband and smile.

"We're so glad you came."

"It's a sad trip, but family is good to see for any reason."

"Isn't it too bad he had to die at Christmas?"

And the widow, a good Christian lady, says, "Because it's Christmas, it is bearable."

Folks begin to drift out, their eyes red, their hugs warm.

～

We go home with brother number four and his wife. They put us up in their daughter's old room with canopied bed and electric, dual-control blanket. She has given us her space, and gone to sleep over with an old high school friend down the street.

We unpack our bags and hang our wrinkled clothes in the closet next to ones she left at home when she went to college. They are long forgotten and long out of style.

It looks like time for a trip to Goodwill.

Everybody in Shannon meets at Goodwill. They drink coffee, find clothes they like in each other's bags, and exchange them before they even get hung up for sale. That's the fun of it.

My sister-in-law and I plan to set aside a couple hours to clean out the closet. We'll get away for a breather and catch up on the gossip.

~

After unpacking our bags, we gather in the den to talk and eat more peanuts. Pretty soon we get to tellin' stories on the five brothers, laughing so hard tears trickle down our cheeks. Healing tears they're called.

Then we open up the storytelling to include relatives not so close.

Seems the mother of one cousin's wife was in Atlanta the week before and had her purse snatched. Being a polite Southern lady, she called after the young man, "Child, I don't have a cent in there, but if you'll wait just a second, I'll write you a check."

We laugh and cry at the same time. It feels good.

Before falling asleep that night I put my arms around my husband and whisper, "How can we be having such a good time at such a sad time?"

~

Next morning we have coffee on the sun porch. Sitting on white wicker furniture, we talk about dividing the African violets left by

Mama after she died. On the wall hangs a picture of little children – black, white and Native American – with an inscription that reads:

> *"Lord, thank you for letting me be born in the South, and for cornbread and turnip greens in my mouth."*

My husband reads recipes from "Southern Living" while squirrels chase each other down the pines and get all crazy jumping into the maze of dogwood branches.

Brother number four's hunting dogs begin to bark for breakfast. I head out to see the new pups. Eight little tails wagging as fast as they can. Eight little mouths learning to bark, surprised by the sounds that come out.

I let myself into their pen, sit on an old blanket and welcome the tumbling balls of fur jumping on top of me. Covered in a pile of six-week-old Brittany Spaniels: what a great way to feel alive! Nothing smells happier than puppy breath. Nothing quite matches being licked by so many velvet tongues.

~

Back inside, we take turns in the bathroom, hoping the hot water will last. I stand in front of the closet and ponder. I'm not sure about my red Christmas suit for the funeral, so I settle on my Black Watch wool in honor of all the Scots in our family.

The First Baptist Church, known as Ol' First, is decorated for Christmas with wreaths, ornaments and crèche scenes loaned each year by members who have too many to put up in their own homes.

A cattle stall has been placed on the grass out front. It faces the road, waiting for people and animals to bring the story alive, but for now it is still empty. On Christmas Eve a high school girl and boy will dress as Mary and Joseph and hold the most recent baby born into the congregation.

Expectant mothers vie for that honor, each hoping their babe will birth in a timely fashion and be swaddled in the manger.

Two cows, a donkey and several sheep will be tethered to a fence surrounding the holy family. Hopefully, it will be sturdier than last year's, when the animals pulled it out of the ground and wandered around the back of the church. One sheep actually got loose and strolled down the center aisle during the pageant. Everybody thought it was planned.

~

The entrance to Ol' First is adorned with Christmas wreaths of boxwood and holly, and some made of shiny green magnolia leaves. Thick, red velvet ribbons have been hot glued at jaunty angles.

Inside, folks have brought their prize Christmas cactus and placed them on bar stools draped in white sheets. Cascades of white and pink and scarlet blossoms fill the narthex.

I stop to admire one plant in particular. Its blossoms hang along stems two feet long, almost touching the floor. It seems to me they are weeping. Norman raised Christmas cactus.

Lunch has been carried into the fellowship hall for the family and their friends: fried chicken, field peas and corn, homemade bread, green Jell-O and canned pear salads, pies and my favorite dessert, Dirt Cake.

This delight is made with Oreo cookie crumbs, cream cheese, chocolate chips, pecans and Cool Whip. It satisfies every chocolate lover's craving. I love the artistic touch of using ceramic, clay pots for the bowl. Each dessert-filled pot holds bouquets of plastic flowers stuck into the "dirt." In the spirit of the season, most are poinsettias.

Desserts are displayed on the last table. Today my motto will be "The last shall be first." After three months on Ultra Slim, my husband and I are in heaven. Our eyes well up again. This time the tears are not from sadness.

I wonder if Norman can taste good things like this where he is now. For the life of me, I can't imagine heaven without dessert. I hope he has Dirt Cake. But just in case he doesn't, I have another helping on him. I figure this is a good way to toast his memory, since Baptists don't drink, at least not publicly.

～

The mother of one of the cousins came early to church. She has a cast on her right arm, from palm to arm pit, and since it takes her longer to get around, she starts fifteen minutes early for every outing. It's a good thing.

Stopping by the ladies' room, she got into a predicament. Just as she pulled her slacks and pantyhose down, the bracelet on her good arm caught in her zipper and she was left in a compromising situation in a locked stall.

Someone she didn't know came into the restroom and they got acquainted real fast. Her new best friend rescued her in time, and she joins the family now as we prepare to walk down the aisle to the front of the sanctuary.

We hold hands by twos and threes, turning to see who came to tell Norman goodbye.

It's the unexpected folks that make the throat catch and the eyes tighten. The gas station attendant who winks as he cleans your windshield; Norman always gave him a tip. The black custodian at the high school, the egg lady, a farmer just outside of town who never fails to call the family when the okra is ready to pick; these are the familiar, everyday faces that touch our hearts.

People turn to watch as we walk down the aisle, and I feel the tenderness in their gaze reaching out to us. They tip their heads in a sad salute. One little boy gives us the thumbs-up sign, and his older sister gets the giggles.

Our eyes feel tight as floodgates. We sisters-in-law worry about our mascara, then feel guilty for worrying about mascara at a time like this. But you can't help thinking about things like that. It makes you feel normal.

∼

The young minister of music stands in front holding a cordless microphone. He looks like a new kid on the block, a little shy and unsure of himself. This is his first funeral.

"Great Is Thy Faithfulness," he sings with heart, which is all anybody cares about anyway.

Then we all sing, "A Mighty Fortress Is Our God." I've never thought about the words much.

> *"Let goods and kindred go,*
> *this mortal life also."*

I guess ol' Luther wrote about other things besides the Reformation in his spare time.

The youngest son sits next to his widowed Mama. On the other side is Susie, their black nursemaid. She's seen the widow's three babies born, helped raise each, and didn't hesitate to tell you which was her favorite and why. Now, two of these children have babies of their own, and the youngest is six weeks from delivering her second.

Everybody holds up real well during the service. Barbara sits dry-eyed, but I notice her hands twisting and untwisting her hankie. The kids cry and pat each other. And finally, the pastor raises his hands for the benediction. You can almost hear a sigh of relief after the final "Amen."

∼

Driving out to the cemetery, Susie warns the expectant mother not to look down into the grave, 'cause it would do something bad to the baby. Old wives' tales may not be particularly helpful, but they make things seem homey and safe.

We had planned to ride to the graveyard with brother number two, but one of the nice young men from the funeral home has an empty limousine and needs company, so we let him carry us to the cemetery.

This part of the South doesn't say "take" or "drive." The word is "carry."

Another thing: they don't cremate here. People in this town bury their dead whole. When I ask one of the brothers about this, he says, "We don't come into the world as a ball of fire. I see no reason to go out as one."

~

Headstones stand high and far apart, with eight-inch letters reminding us of folks named McLaughlin, McRae, McNeil, Graham, McCloud, and McGowan. Bright Christmas wreaths hang on marble gravestones, making bold affirmations of joy to the world.

We stand around the casket for the twenty-third Psalm and a prayer. Then folks mingle, with tears and talk and comfort, Southern style. I started to say "Southern Comfort", but remembered again we are with Baptists.

We girls…

Now I have to digress just a bit, to say that Southern women are "girls" until they die. I guess some things haven't made their way south yet, like cremation and gender awareness. Inclusive language is considered something the carpetbaggers thought up. "Y'all" is about as inclusive as they get here. From my point of view, it's kinda sweet to be called a girl after fifty. I get used to it real easy. So, we sisters are "girls" and the brothers left are "boys."

Norman isn't called a "boy" anymore. I guess you finally grow up when you die.

~

Anyway, back to us girls at the cemetery getting cramps in our calves, balancing on our toes, trying to keep our high heels from sinking into the damp earth.

We talk and talk, cry and cry, hug and kiss, and start all over again.

The little girl who lives across the street from Norman, the one who sent a single, red rose to the funeral home, is here in her new purple coat, opened before Christmas just for this. I tell her how much Norman would have liked her rose. From all the flower sprays, her gift was chosen to sit next to Norman's photograph by the casket.

She carries a little white lace handkerchief. I haven't seen one of these since my high school prom. Mother loaned me her hankie, as she called it, but warned me: "Hankies are for showing; tissues are for blowing. If you really need to blow your nose, I've tucked a tissue in your purse."

～

I watch lots of folks at the ceremony blowing their noses on white, linen handkerchiefs. They are crying for Norman's being gone, and the family missing him so much, but crying about other things too.

They cry for their own losses. Some of their own folks died this year. Some cry because this is their first Christmas alone: not necessarily from a death – maybe from divorce, separation, or Alzheimer's. They cry because they've been asked to retire early, or their kids aren't talking to them, or they love someone who won't live to celebrate next Christmas.

Each of us cries for Norman and each of us cries for ourselves. We share a fellowship of sorrow, and feel closer this Christmas than many in the past. I wonder: is it sadness, rather than gladness, that is the "blest tie that binds?"

∼

Cardinals swoop from pine to pine, looking like scarlet Christmas ornaments being tossed back and forth by children while their parents decorate the family tree.

Finally, we can't hug anymore. Tears begin to dry, leaving us girls with red eyes, damp handkerchiefs and mascara-smudged tissues stuffed up our sleeves.

It's time to go by the widow's house. "Barbara's house," I call it for the first time. It has always been "Barbara and Norman's."

Strange how you have to modify your language after someone dies. Barbara will have to use *mine* instead of *ours*, and *I* instead of *we*. I wonder how long that will take her. There are so many changes she will discover in her new, single life.

~

When we arrive at Barbara's house, it is stuffed with food. Sixty-some casseroles and platters had come before the funeral, and it looks like more snuck in the back while we were at the graveyard.

It takes one person standing by the front door just to write down all the names, while others look for places to put it all. Every countertop, table and appliance is covered with casseroles, and the air fills up with that delicious smell of cholesterol.

First, we have to taste the food brought by friends who are eating with us. They need to hear us ooh and aah. Then we have to eat more – and fast – to keep up with the parade of love offerings.

The next-door neighbor says we can use the extra freezer she keeps in her garage. It is my job to be sure each dish has someone's name taped on the bottom. I hope Barbara won't have to return all of these bowls in person. Maybe she can throw a "come-get-your-casserole" tea party in a month or so.

The long December night slips into Barbara's yard. Older widow friends slip out her front door to find their cars and get home while it is still light.

It seems like a good night to turn in early. Each of us grabs a casserole or two and takes them to the freezer next door before we head to our beds. Before leaving, I have to taste another Dirt Pie someone brought into the screened porch and left on a card table.

No name on the bottom of the pot. Guess this one can actually be planted up next spring. I'll send Barbara some hyacinth bulbs. They were my dad's favorite. He used to quote a Persian poet:

> *Shouldest thou repair to thy larder and find yet two loaves remain, yet I would counsel thee to sell one, and buy white hyacinths to feed thy soul.*

~

Next day the oldest grandbaby gets sick to her tummy. Several of the adults develop the same symptoms. At first we think it is from eating too much rich food.

Then a couple of the cousins who ate very little (and were mighty glad of that) come down with the same bug. It hits some at one end and others at the other. A few burn the candle at both ends.

I am spared. Still feeling pretty good at noon the next day, my sister-in-law and I head for Goodwill, our arms full of clothes, high school leftovers, hangers and all. It takes two cars to clear things out, because once our bedroom closet is empty, we find a storage room full of grade school leftovers.

Somebody suggests we save them for grandchildren. "Good grief!" we sigh, and head out the door with a second load.

~

Goodwill sees us coming and puts on the coffee pot. Folks who know us come out and ask how Barbara is doing today. We say she's holding up, but I suggest she will need some friends to drop-in during the next few weeks.

Everyone wonders what she will do on Christmas day. I realize we haven't given this any thought. Turns out her neighbors have.

"Well, what with those grandchildren around, I imagine she'll be warming up lots of casseroles, watching her family open presents, cleaning up torn wrapping paper and winding up ribbon to use next Christmas."

"She has plenty of Christmas cookies, enough to feed the grade school. Maybe she'll let the kids have a big party with their friends. The weather is supposed to be good through the New Year, so they can drop their crumbs outside."

"We've been wanting to start a book club for years. This might be a great time to start one. Do you think Barbara would like to host the group at her house?"

As I listen to Barbara's friends organize her life for the next few months, I know she will come through this season of sadness with plenty of company.

~

Sister-in-law reminds me we need to get back to the house and dress for the Christmas Eve musical.

I am so fueled on caffeine, I can't stop saying goodbye. I'll wave and turn to go, only to think of one more question:

"Who did that snooty cheerleader in your class finally marry?"

"Did the music teacher get fired for wearing those see-through blouses?"

"Why did they ask the last preacher to leave? I thought he was doing such a great job."

Sister-in-law grabs my sleeve and pulls me through the door, promising she'll answer the rest of my questions on the way home.

$\sim$

I'm not sure what to wear to the musical. Perhaps it is time for the red suit.

The funeral is over. Christmas is tomorrow. Red works.

We drive through town on our way to church, past Gone-with-the-Wind houses burning one white candle in each window, and rainbow Christmas trees refracting through beveled glass. There is deep silence in the car.

Norman was a man acquainted with silence. He could sit in a porch swing surrounded by family and say nothing for an hour or two, yet his unspoken conversation made even me feel at home.

~

Carols ring through the candlelight at Ol' First. Hurricane lamps flicker. We hold hands. Norman would have loved this night.

Barbara sits with her children. Her only daughter sits especially close, and during "Silent Night, Holy Night," she reaches over, takes her mama's hand and places it on her belly. The widow's grandbaby is kicking. This Christmas, the widow's own Mary is great with child.

We all sing, "Hark the Herald Angels Sing" as a final carol.

> *Born that man no more may die,*
> *born to raise the sons of earth,*
> *born to give them second birth.*

I never knew until now, how well the songs of Christmas speak to grieving folk.

∼

We leave Shannon the next day, knowing it will be awhile before we come back.

"Maybe next summer," we say.

Folks wave and call, "Come back now, y'all, hear?"

"We love you."

"Bye now."

"And Merry Christmas!"

And strangely enough, it is.

About the Author

Sylvia Casberg attended San Francisco Theological Seminary as a second career student. She received her Master of Divinity and Doctor of Ministry degrees there.

After fourteen years serving Wellshire Presbyterian Church, in Denver, CO, she became Chaplain of the Moscow Protestant Chaplaincy in Russia, from 1995 to 1996. Returning to the States, Sylvia was called as a chaplain to the University of Colorado Hospital shortly before 9/11.

The birth of Sylvia's grandson called her to California in 2005. Here she served as Associate Pastor at Bethania Lutheran Church, in Solvang. She is now retired and writing full time.